The Holy Communion

ALSO CALLED THE EUCHARIST
AND THE LORD'S SUPPER

The Holy Communion
FIRST ORDER

© The Anglican Church of Australia Trust Corporation 1995

Apart from any fair dealing for the purposes of private study, research, criticism or review, as permitted under the Copyright Act, no part may be reproduced by any process without written permission from the publisher.

Published by Broughton Publishing P/L
Your National Anglican Publisher
32 Glenvale Crescent
Mulgrave Victoria 3170
Australia

www.broughtonpublishing.com.au

ISBN 987-1-8763085-4-4
An extract from *A Prayer Book for Australia*
Reprints 1998, 1999, 2001, 2006, 2008, 2010, 2011

Texts are based on *An Australian Prayer Book* 1978 and its sources or are original work by the Liturgical Commission. The English translation of The Lord's Prayer, Kyrie Eleison, Gloria in Excelsis, The Nicene Creed, Sursum Corda, Sanctus and Benedictus, Agnus Dei are those prepared by the English Language Liturgical Consultation (ELLC) 1988.

Scripture passages are based on the *Revised Standard Version of the Bible* © 1946, 1952, 1971, 1973 and the *New Revised Standard Version of the Bible* © 1989 by the Division of Christian Education of the National Council of Churches of Christ in the USA.

Notice Pagination corresponds with *A Prayer Book for Australia* and options, normally omitted, are indicated by grey marginal shading.

Printed in Australia

Broughton Publishing uses paper made from wood pulp of managed forests, thereby renewing natural resources.

GATHERING IN GOD'S NAME

1   *A psalm, hymn or anthem may be sung when the ministers enter.*

The priest may begin the service at the prayer desk, or at some other convenient place.

2   *The priest may greet the people.*

The Lord be with you.
And also with you.

3   *A Sentence of Scripture appropriate to the day may be read.*

4   *The people kneeling, this Prayer of Preparation is said by the priest, or the priest and people together.*

Let us pray.
Almighty God,
to whom all hearts are open,
all desires known,
and from whom no secrets are hidden:
cleanse the thoughts of our hearts
by the inspiration of your Holy Spirit,
that we may perfectly love you,
and worthily magnify your holy name,
through Christ our Lord. **Amen.**

5   *The priest reads aloud the commandments. They may be read as a continuous passage, or after each commandment except the last the people may answer*

**Lord, have mercy on us:
and incline our hearts to keep this law.**

Hear the commandments which God gave his people Israel.

1   I am the Lord your God who brought you out of the land of slavery; you shall have no other gods but me.
2   You shall not make for yourself a graven image, or any likeness of anything that is in heaven above, or that is on the earth beneath, or that is in the water under the earth; you shall not bow down to them or serve them.

3   You shall not take the name of the Lord your God in vain.
4   Remember the sabbath day to keep it holy. Six days shall you labour and do all you have to do, but the seventh day is the sabbath of the Lord your God.
5   Honour your father and your mother.
6   You shall do no murder.
7   You shall not commit adultery.
8   You shall not steal.
9   You shall not bear false witness against your neighbour.
10 You shall not covet anything that is your neighbour's.

Lord, have mercy on us: and write your law in our hearts by your Holy Spirit.

Or this

'Hear, O Israel: the Lord our God, the Lord is one; you shall love the Lord your God with all your heart, and with all your soul, and with all your mind, and with all your strength.' Jesus said: 'This is the great and first commandment. And a second is like it: You shall love your neighbour as yourself.'

Lord, have mercy on us: and write your law in our hearts by your Holy Spirit.

6   *The priest says*

Let us pray.

and then says the Collect of the Day.

THE MINISTRY OF THE WORD

7 *A Reading or Readings from the Bible, as appointed.*

Each is introduced,

The reading from ..., chapter ... beginning at verse ...,

and at the end, the reader may say

Hear the word of the Lord,
thanks be to God.

8 *A psalm, hymn, or canticle may be said or sung between the readings.*

9 *The people stand for the Gospel, which is introduced*

The gospel of our Lord Jesus Christ, according to...
[chapter...verse...]

The people may respond

Glory to you, Lord Jesus Christ.

After the Gospel the reader says

This is the Gospel of the Lord,

or [For] the Gospel of the Lord,
praise to you, Lord Jesus Christ.

10 *The Sermon is preached here, or after the creed.*

11 *The Nicene Creed is said or sung, all standing.*
It may be omitted on weekdays.

We believe in one God,
the Father, the almighty,
maker of heaven and earth,
of all that is, seen and unseen.

We believe in one Lord, Jesus Christ,
   the only Son of God,
   eternally begotten of the Father,
   God from God, Light from Light,
   true God from true God,
   begotten, not made,
   of one Being with the Father;
   through him all things were made.
   For us and for our salvation
   he came down from heaven,
   was incarnate of the Holy Spirit and the virgin Mary
   and became truly human.
   For our sake he was crucified under Pontius Pilate;
   he suffered death and was buried.
   On the third day he rose again
   in accordance with the Scriptures;
   he ascended into heaven
   and is seated at the right hand of the Father.
   He will come again in glory to judge
      the living and the dead,
   and his kingdom will have no end.
We believe in the Holy Spirit, the Lord, the giver of life,
   who proceeds from the Father and the Son,
   who with the Father and the Son
      is worshipped and glorified,
   who has spoken through the prophets.
   We believe in one holy catholic and apostolic Church.
   We acknowledge one baptism for the
      forgiveness of sins.
   We look for the resurrection of the dead,
   and the life of the world to come. Amen.

12   *The Sermon is preached here if it has not been preached earlier.*

THE OFFERTORY

13   The priest begins the Offertory, saying one or more of these sentences.

Let your light so shine that others may see your good works and give glory to your Father in heaven.
Matthew 5.16

Do not store up for yourselves treasures on earth, where moth and rust consume and where thieves break in and steal: but store up for yourselves treasures in heaven, where neither moth nor rust consume, and thieves do not break in and steal. For where your treasure is, there your heart will be also.
Matthew 6.19–20

Not everyone who says to me, 'Lord, Lord', will enter the kingdom of heaven, but whoever does the will of my Father who is in heaven.
Matthew 7.21

Whenever we have opportunity, let us do good to all, and especially to those of the household of faith.
Galatians 6.10

Do not neglect to do good and to share what you have, for such sacrifices are pleasing to God.
Hebrews 13.16

Whoever sows sparingly will also reap sparingly; whoever sows bountifully will also reap bountifully. Each of you must give as you have made up your mind, not reluctantly or under compulsion, for God loves a cheerful giver.
2 Corinthians 9.6–7

How does God's love abide in anyone who has this world's goods, sees a brother or sister in need, and yet refuses help?
1 John 3.17

Offer to God a sacrifice of thanksgiving, pay your vows to the Most High. Those who bring thanksgiving as their sacrifice honour me. To those who go the right way I will show the salvation of God.
Psalm 50.14, 23

Through Christ, then, let us continually offer a sacrifice of praise to God, that is, the fruit of lips that confess his name.

Hebrews 13.15

14 *While these sentences are being read, the alms and other offerings of the people are collected and brought to the priest who reverently presents and places them on the Holy Table.*

A hymn may also be sung during the collection.

When there is a communion, the priest then places sufficient bread and wine on the table.

THE PRAYERS

15 *The minister may bid special prayers and thanksgivings.*

The Intercession is then said.

If there are no alms or oblations, the words in italics in the first paragraph of this prayer are omitted.

Let us pray for all people, and for the Church throughout the world.

Almighty and everliving God, we are taught by your holy apostle to make prayers and supplications and to give thanks for all people: we ask you in your mercy *[to accept our alms and oblations and]* to receive our prayers which we offer to your divine majesty.

We pray that you will lead the nations of the world in the ways of righteousness and peace, and guide their rulers in wisdom and justice for the tranquillity and good of all. Bless especially your servant Elizabeth our Queen, her representatives and ministers, her parliaments, and all who exercise authority in this land. Grant that they may impartially administer justice, restrain wickedness and vice, and uphold integrity and truth.

We beseech you to inspire continually the universal Church with the spirit of truth, unity, and concord; and grant that all who confess your holy name may agree in the truth of your holy word, and live in unity and godly love.

Give grace, heavenly Father, to all bishops and other ministers (especially N our bishop and...), that, by their life and doctrine, they may set forth your true, life-giving word, and rightly and duly administer your holy sacraments. And to all your people give your heavenly grace, and especially to this congregation here present, that they may receive your word with meek hearts and due reverence and serve you in holiness and righteousness all the days of their life.

We ask you of your goodness, Lord, to comfort and sustain all who in this transitory life are in trouble, sorrow, need, sickness, or any other adversity.

We also bless your holy name for all your servants who have died in the faith of Christ. Give us grace to follow their good examples, that with them we may be partakers of your heavenly kingdom.

Grant this, Father, for Jesus Christ's sake, our only mediator and advocate. **Amen.**

16 *A hymn may be sung.*

PREPARATION FOR THE LORD'S SUPPER

17   This exhortation may be read.

Brothers and sisters in Christ, we who would come to the holy communion of the body and blood of our Saviour Christ must consider how St Paul exhorts us to examine ourselves before presuming to eat of that bread and drink of that cup.

For the benefit is great, if with a penitent heart and lively faith we receive that holy sacrament. We then spiritually eat the flesh of Christ and drink his blood; we dwell in Christ and he in us; we are one with Christ and Christ with us.

Yet also the danger is great, if we receive the bread and cup unworthily. Judge yourselves therefore, that you be not judged of the Lord. Repent truly of your sins, having a steadfast faith in Christ our Saviour. Amend your lives and love your neighbour.

Above all, give hearty thanks to God for the redemption of the world by the death and passion of our Saviour Christ, truly God and truly human, who humbled himself to death on the cross for us sinners, that he might make us children of God, and raise us to eternal life.

or

Brothers and sisters in Christ, we who come to receive the holy communion of the body and blood of our Saviour Christ can come only because of his great love for us. For, although we are completely undeserving of his love, yet in order to raise us from the darkness of death to everlasting life as God's sons and daughters, our Saviour Christ humbled himself to share our life and to die for us on the cross. In remembrance of his death, and as a pledge of his love, Jesus instituted this holy sacrament which we are now to share.

But those who would eat the bread and drink the cup of the Lord must examine themselves, and amend their lives. They must come with a penitent heart and steadfast faith. Above all they must give thanks to God for his love towards us in Christ Jesus.

18 The minister continues

You who truly and earnestly repent of your sins, and are in love and charity with your neighbours, and intend to lead a new life, following the commandments of God and walking in his holy ways, draw near with faith, and take this holy sacrament to strengthen and comfort you. But first, let us make a humble confession of our sins to almighty God.

19 A pause for self-examination may be observed.

All then say this General Confession.

Almighty God, Father of our Lord Jesus Christ,
maker of all things, judge of all people,
we acknowledge with shame the sins we have committed,
by thought, word, and deed, against your divine majesty,
provoking most justly your wrath and indignation
   against us.
We earnestly repent, and are heartily sorry
   for all our misdoings.
Have mercy on us, most merciful Father.
For your Son our Lord Jesus Christ's sake
forgive us all that is past,
and grant that we may ever hereafter
   serve and please you in newness of life,
to the honour and glory of your name,
through Jesus Christ our Lord. Amen.

20 The priest, or bishop if present, stands and pronounces this Absolution.

Almighty God our heavenly Father, who of his great mercy has promised forgiveness of sins to all who with hearty repentance and true faith turn to him: have mercy on you; pardon and deliver you from all your sins; confirm and strengthen you in all goodness; and keep you in eternal life; through Jesus Christ our Lord. **Amen.**

THE LORD'S SUPPER

21   The Words of Assurance

One or more of these sentences is said.

Hear the words of assurance for those who truly turn to Christ:

Jesus said: Come to me, all who labour and are heavy laden, and I will give you rest.

Matthew 11.28

God so loved the world that he gave his only Son, that whoever believes in him should not perish but have eternal life.

John 3.16

The saying is sure and worthy of full acceptance, that Christ Jesus came into the world to save sinners.

1 Timothy 1.15

If any one sins, we have an advocate with the Father, Jesus Christ the righteous; and he is the perfect offering for our sins.

1 John 2.1, 2

22   The priest then begins the Thanksgiving and Communion.

Lift up your hearts.
We lift them to the Lord.
Let us give thanks to the Lord our God.
It is right to give our thanks and praise.

It is indeed right, and our bounden duty, that we should at all times and in all places give thanks to you, Lord, Mighty Creator, and Eternal God.

On certain days a special preface is said here (see ¶ 23 below).

Therefore with angels and archangels, and with the whole company of heaven, we proclaim your great and glorious name, evermore praising you, and saying:

Holy, holy, holy, Lord God of hosts,
heaven and earth are full of your glory.
Glory to you, O Lord most high.

23 Special prefaces

Christmas, Presentation, Annunciation

And now we praise you because you gave your only Son Jesus Christ to be born for us. By the power of the Holy Spirit he was conceived of the virgin Mary his mother; being himself without sin, to make us clean from all sin.

Easter season

But chiefly are we bound to praise you for the glorious resurrection of your Son Jesus Christ our Lord. He is the true passover lamb who was offered for us and has taken away the sin of the world. By his death he has destroyed death; by his rising to life again he has restored to us eternal life.

Ascension

We praise you through our Lord Jesus Christ, who was seen by his disciples after his glorious resurrection and in their sight ascended into heaven to prepare a place for us, that where he is we might also be and reign with him in glory.

Whitsunday/Pentecost

We praise you through our Lord Jesus Christ, for, in accordance with his promise, the Holy Spirit came down from heaven upon the apostles, to teach them and to lead them into all truth; giving them power and boldness with fervent zeal to preach the gospel to all nations, by which we have been brought out of darkness into the true knowledge of you and of your Son Jesus Christ.

Trinity

For you are one God, one Lord, three Persons in one God. For all that we believe of your glory, Father, we believe equally of the glory of your Son and of the Holy Spirit. We worship you, one God in Trinity and Trinity in unity.

Dedication festival and other occasions

We praise you through Jesus Christ our Lord, the true high priest who has cleansed us from sin and made us a royal priesthood called to serve you for ever.

Saints' days

We praise you for the example and encouragement of your saints; for their witness to the truth of your gospel; and for the hope of glory which we share with them in Jesus Christ our Lord.

24 *Then the priest, kneeling down at the Lord's Table, says this prayer in the name of all who are to receive the communion (or all may join in saying the prayer).*

We do not presume
to come to your table, merciful Lord,
trusting in our own righteousness,
but in your manifold and great mercies.
We are not worthy
so much as to gather up the crumbs under your table.
But you are the same Lord
whose nature is always to have mercy.
Grant us, therefore, gracious Lord,
so to eat the flesh of your dear Son Jesus Christ,
and to drink his blood,
that we may evermore dwell in him,
and he in us. **Amen.**

25 *The priest arranges the bread and wine so that they may be taken, and the bread broken, in the sight of the people. The priest says the Prayer of Consecration.*

All glory to you, our heavenly Father, for in your tender mercy you gave your only Son Jesus Christ to suffer death on the cross for our redemption: who made there, by his one oblation of himself once offered, a full, perfect, and sufficient sacrifice, oblation and satisfaction for the sins of the whole world; and instituted, and in his holy gospel commanded us to continue, a perpetual memory of his precious death until his coming again.

Hear us, merciful Father, we humbly pray, and grant that we who receive these gifts of your creation, this bread and this wine, according to your Son our Saviour Jesus Christ's holy institution, in remembrance of his death and passion, may be partakers of his most blessed body and blood; who on the night he was betrayed took bread[1], and when he had given you thanks, he broke it[2], and gave it to his disciples, saying, 'Take, eat[3]; this is my body which is given for you; do this in remembrance of me.' Likewise after supper he took the cup[4], and when he had given thanks, he gave it to them saying, 'Drink from this, all of you[5]; for this is my blood of the New Testament, which is shed for you and for many for the remission of sins; do this, as often as you drink it, in remembrance of me.'

All answer **Amen.**

[1] *Here the Priest is to take the bread.*
[2] *Here to break the bread.*
[3] *Here to lay hands on all the bread.*
[4] *Here the Priest is to take the cup.*
[5] *And here to indicate every vessel (be it chalice or flagon) in which there is any wine to be consecrated.*

26 *The priest receives the communion in both kinds and then proceeds to distribute it to any bishops, priests, and deacons who are present, and then to the people in their hands as they kneel.*

The minister gives the bread, saying

The body of our Lord Jesus Christ, which was given for you, preserve your body and soul to everlasting life; take and eat this in remembrance that Christ died for you, and feed on him in your heart by faith with thanksgiving.

The minister gives the cup, saying

The blood of our Lord Jesus Christ, which was shed for you, preserve your body and soul to everlasting life; drink this in remembrance that Christ's blood was shed for you, and be thankful.

27 *If the consecrated bread or wine prove insufficient for the communion, the priest is to consecrate more, beginning at 'Our Saviour Christ on the night ...' for the bread and at 'Likewise after supper ...' for the cup.*

28 *When all have received, the minister reverently places on the table what remains of the consecrated elements, covering it with a fair linen cloth.*

AFTER COMMUNION

29   The priest says

Let us pray.

[As our Saviour Christ has taught us, we are confident to pray:]

Our Father in heaven,
  hallowed be your name,
  your kingdom come,
  your will be done,
    on earth as in heaven.
Give us today our daily bread.
Forgive us our sins
  as we forgive those who sin against us.
Save us from the time of trial,
  and deliver us from evil.
For the kingdom, the power, and the glory are yours
now and for ever. Amen.

30   Then is said

Lord and heavenly Father, we your humble servants entirely desire your fatherly goodness mercifully to accept this our sacrifice of praise and thanksgiving, and to grant that, by the merits and death of your Son Jesus Christ, and through faith in his blood, we and your whole Church may receive forgiveness of our sins and all other benefits of his passion. And here we offer and present to you, O Lord, ourselves, our souls and bodies, to be a reasonable, holy, and living sacrifice, humbly beseeching you that all we who are partakers of this holy communion may be fulfilled with your grace and heavenly benediction.

And although we are unworthy, through our many sins, to offer you any sacrifice, yet we pray that you will accept this, our bounden duty and service, not weighing our merits but pardoning our offences, through Jesus Christ our Lord; by whom and with whom, in the unity of the Holy Spirit, all honour and glory are yours, Father, world without end. **Amen.**

or

Almighty and everliving God, we heartily thank you that you graciously feed us, who have duly received these holy mysteries, with the spiritual food of the most precious body and blood of your Son our Saviour Jesus Christ, and thus assure us of your favour and goodness towards us and that we are true members of the mystical body of your Son, the blessed company of all faithful people, and are also heirs, through hope, of your eternal kingdom, by the merits of the most precious death and passion of your dear Son.
And we humbly beseech you, heavenly Father, so to assist us with your grace, that we may continue in that holy fellowship, and do all such good works as you have prepared for us to walk in, through Jesus Christ our Lord, to whom with you and the Holy Spirit be all honour and glory, world without end. **Amen.**

31   *This Hymn of Praise (Gloria in excelsis) is said or sung.*

**Glory to God in the highest
and peace to God's people on earth.
Lord God, heavenly King,
almighty God and Father,
    we worship you, we give you thanks,
    we praise you for your glory.
Lord Jesus Christ, only Son of the Father,
Lord God, Lamb of God,
    you take away the sin of the world:
        have mercy on us;
    you are seated at the right hand of the Father:
        receive our prayer.
For you alone are the Holy One;
you alone are the Lord;
you alone are the Most High,
    Jesus Christ,
    with the Holy Spirit,
    in the glory of God the Father. Amen.**

32 *The priest, or bishop if present, lets the people depart with this Blessing.*

The peace of God which passes all understanding, keep your hearts and minds in the knowledge and love of God, and of his Son Jesus Christ our Lord; and the blessing of God Almighty, the Father, the Son, and the Holy Spirit, be amongst you, and remain with you always. **Amen**

33 *If any of the consecrated bread and wine remain, it shall not be carried out of the church, but the priest (and other communicants asked by the priest if required) shall reverently eat and drink the same immediately after the Blessing.*

Notes

1. The reader may preface the announcement of the Gospel with the salutation, 'The Lord be with you', to which the people respond, **'And also with you'**.
2. The sermon may be omitted on weekdays.
3. Formal notices may be given before the service begins, before the sermon, after the Nicene Creed, or after the intercession.
4. The versicle and response, 'Lord, in your mercy, **hear our prayer'** may be used between the paragraphs in the intercession at ¶ 15.
5. For the significance of kneeling to receive the Lord's Supper, see the declaration which is printed at the conclusion of the Communion service in *The Book of Common Prayer*, and note 4 on page 822.

The Holy Communion
SECOND ORDER

GATHERING IN GOD'S NAME

1. *A psalm, hymn, or anthem may be sung when the ministers enter or after the greeting. A seasonal sentence may be used here or after ¶ 3.*

2. *An Invocation, or an Acclamation such as follows, may be said before or after the greeting.*

Blessed be God: Father, Son and Holy Spirit.
Blessed be God's kingdom, now and for ever.

In Lent and on other penitential occasions

Bless the Lord who forgives all our sins,
whose mercy endures for ever.

3. *The Greeting. The priest greets the people in these or other suitable words.*

The grace of the Lord Jesus Christ, and the love of God, and the fellowship of the Holy Spirit, be with you all.
And also with you.

or

The Lord be with you.
And also with you.

or

From Easter Day to Pentecost

Christ is risen. [Alleluia.]
He is risen indeed. [Alleluia.]

4. *This Prayer of Preparation may be said.*

[Let us pray.]
**Almighty God,
to whom all hearts are open,
all desires known,
and from whom no secrets are hidden:
cleanse the thoughts of our hearts
by the inspiration of your Holy Spirit,
that we may perfectly love you,
and worthily magnify your holy name,
through Christ our Lord. Amen.**

¶ 5 to 10 may be used according to local and seasonal custom, in any appropriate form and sequence.

5   *The Two Great Commandments, the Ten Commandments (see page 101), or other suitable passages are said when the confession follows.*

'Hear, O Israel, the Lord our God, the Lord is one; you shall love the Lord your God with all your heart, and with all your soul, and with all your mind, and with all your strength.' Jesus said: 'This is the great and first commandment. And a second is like it: you shall love your neighbour as yourself.'

6   *A deacon or other minister may introduce the Confession with a seasonal introduction (see pages 147–63) or other suitable words.*

Silence may be kept.

Let us confess our sins in penitence and faith, confident in God's forgiveness.
Merciful God,
our maker and our judge,
we have sinned against you
in thought, word, and deed,
  and in what we have failed to do:
we have not loved you with our whole heart;
we have not loved our neighbours as ourselves;
we repent, and are sorry for all our sins.
Father, forgive us.
Strengthen us to love and obey you
  in newness of life;
through Jesus Christ our Lord. Amen.

7   *The Absolution. Standing, the priest says*

Almighty God,
who has promised forgiveness to all who turn to him in faith:
pardon you and set you free from all your sins,
strengthen you in all goodness
and keep you in eternal life,
through Jesus Christ our Lord. **Amen.**

8   *'Lord, have mercy' (Kyrie eleison)*

Lord, have mercy	**Kyrie eleison**
Christ, have mercy	**Christe eleison**
Lord, have mercy	**Kyrie eleison**

9 *The Hymn of Praise, Gloria in excelsis. It may be omitted during Advent and Lent (see note 4).*

Glory to God in the highest,
and peace to God's people on earth.
Lord God, heavenly King,
almighty God and Father,
   we worship you, we give you thanks,
   we praise you for your glory.
Lord Jesus Christ, only Son of the Father,
   Lord God, Lamb of God,
   you take away the sin of the world:
      have mercy on us;
   you are seated at the right hand of the Father:
      receive our prayer.
For you alone are the Holy One,
you alone are the Lord,
you alone are the Most High
   Jesus Christ,
   with the Holy Spirit,
   in the glory of God the Father. Amen.

10 *Especially during Advent and Lent, the following (Trisagion) may be said.*

Holy God, holy and mighty, holy and immortal,
have mercy on us.

11 *The Collect of the Day*

   The priest says

Let us pray.

   The community may pray silently.

   The priest says or sings the collect.

THE MINISTRY OF THE WORD

12 *All sit for the Reading from the Old Testament or as appointed.*
    After each reading the reader may say

Hear the word of the Lord,
thanks be to God.

Silence may follow each reading.

13 *A Psalm, hymn or anthem may be sung.*
14 *The Reading from the New Testament (other than from the gospels).*
15 *A hymn or anthem may be sung.*
16 *All stand for the Gospel Reading.*
    The deacon or other reader may say

The Lord be with you.
And also with you.

The reader says

The Gospel of our Lord Jesus Christ according to…
[chapter… verse…]
Glory to you Lord Jesus Christ.

After the Gospel, the reader says

This is the Gospel of the Lord,
or [For] the Gospel of the Lord,
Praise to you Lord Jesus Christ.

17 *The Sermon*

    Silence may follow.

18 *On Sundays the Nicene Creed or the Apostles' Creed (see page 171) is said or sung, all standing.*

*[The minister may say these or similar words.
Let us together affirm the faith of the Church:]*
We believe in one God,
   the Father, the almighty,
   maker of heaven and earth,
   of all that is, seen and unseen.
We believe in one Lord, Jesus Christ,
   the only Son of God,
   eternally begotten of the Father,
   God from God, Light from Light,
   true God from true God,
   begotten, not made,
   of one being with the Father;
   through him all things were made.
   For us and for our salvation
   he came down from heaven,
   was incarnate of the Holy Spirit and the virgin Mary
   and became truly human.
   For our sake he was crucified under Pontius Pilate;
   he suffered death and was buried.
   On the third day he rose again
   in accordance with the Scriptures;
   he ascended into heaven
   and is seated at the right hand of the Father.
   He will come again in glory to judge
      the living and the dead
   and his kingdom will have no end.
We believe in the Holy Spirit, the Lord, the giver of life,
   who proceeds from the Father and the Son,
   who with the Father and the Son
   is worshipped and glorified,
   who has spoken through the prophets.
   We believe in one holy catholic and apostolic Church.
   We acknowledge one baptism for the
      forgiveness of sins.
   We look for the resurrection of the dead,
   and the life of the world to come. Amen.

THE PRAYERS OF THE PEOPLE

19 *The minister says*

Let us pray for the world and for the Church.

The prayers may be offered by a deacon and/or other members of the congregation.

Periods of silence may be kept.

Intercessions and thanksgivings may end with an appropriate response, for example:

Lord, in your mercy,
hear our prayer.

Lord, hear us.
Lord, hear our prayer.

Father, hear our prayer
through Jesus Christ our Lord.

Let us pray to the Lord.
Lord, have mercy.

For your love and goodness
we give you thanks, O God.

God of grace,
hear our prayer.

For suitable patterns of prayer, see pages 172–73, 183–87.

The prayers may conclude with this or another suitable prayer.

Almighty God, you have promised to hear our prayers.
Grant that what we have asked in faith
we may by your grace receive,
through Jesus Christ our Lord. Amen.

or, unless the Lord's Prayer is used later, the minister may say

Accept our prayers through Jesus Christ our Lord, who taught us to pray,
Our Father in heaven,
   hallowed be your name,
   your kingdom come,
   your will be done,
     on earth as in heaven.
Give us today our daily bread.
Forgive us our sins
   as we forgive those who sin against us.
Save us from the time of trial
   and deliver us from evil.
For the kingdom, the power, and the glory are yours
now and for ever. Amen.

[PREPARATION]

20 *A selection from the following or other suitable sentences of Scripture may be used.*

Jesus said: Come to me all who labour and are heavy laden, and I will give you rest.
Matthew 11.28

Jesus said: I am the bread of life. Whoever comes to me will never be hungry, and whoever believes in me will never be thirsty.
John 6.35

Jesus said: A new commandment I give to you, that you love one another, even as I have loved you.
John 13.34

Whenever you stand praying, forgive, if you have anything against any one; so that your Father also who is in heaven may forgive you your trespasses.
Mark 11.25

God so loved the world that he gave his only Son, that whoever believes in him should not perish but have eternal life.
John 3.16

and/or

21 *This Prayer of Approach may be used.*

[Let us pray.]

**We do not presume
to come to your table, merciful Lord,
trusting in our own righteousness,
but in your manifold and great mercies.
We are not worthy
so much as to gather up the crumbs under your table.
But you are the same Lord
whose nature is always to have mercy.
Grant us, therefore, gracious Lord,
so to eat the flesh of your dear Son Jesus Christ,
and to drink his blood,
that we may evermore dwell in him,
and he in us. Amen.**

CONFESSION AND ABSOLUTION

22 *At least on Sundays and other Holy Days a general Confession is said here if it has not been said at ¶ 6.*

The deacon or other minister introduces the confession with the following, a seasonal introduction (pages 147–63) or other suitable words such as an exhortation (page 108), 1 Corinthians 11.26–28 or Isaiah 55.6–8.

God is steadfast in love and infinite in mercy, welcoming sinners and inviting them to the Lord's table.

Silence may be kept.

Let us confess our sins in penitence and faith, confident in God's forgiveness.

**Merciful God,
our maker and our judge,
we have sinned against you in thought, word, and deed,
   and in what we have failed to do:
we have not loved you with our whole heart;
we have not loved our neighbours as ourselves;
we repent, and are sorry for all our sins.
Father, forgive us.
Strengthen us to love and obey you in newness of life;
through Jesus Christ our Lord. Amen.**

23 *The Absolution. Standing, the priest says*

Almighty God,
who has promised forgiveness to all who turn to him in faith:
pardon you and set you free from all your sins,
strengthen you in all goodness
and keep you in eternal life,
through Jesus Christ our Lord. **Amen.**

THE GREETING OF PEACE

24 *All stand. The Greeting of Peace is introduced with these or other suitable words.*

We are the body of Christ.
His Spirit is with us.

or

Christ has reconciled us to God in one body by the cross.
We meet in his name and share his peace.

The priest says

The peace of the Lord be always with you.
And also with you.

All may exchange a sign of peace.

A hymn may be sung.

25 *The gifts of the people are brought to the Lord's Table. They may be presented in silence or a suitable prayer, such as follows, may be used.*

Blessed are you, Lord, God of all creation.
Through your goodness we have these gifts to share.
Accept and use our offerings for your glory
and for the service of your kingdom.
Blessed be God for ever.

THE GREAT THANKSGIVING

26 *The priest takes the bread and wine for the communion, places them on the Lord's Table, and says the following (Thanksgiving 1) or another authorised Prayer of Thanksgiving and Consecration.*

Additional Thanksgivings

Thanksgiving 2 page 130
Thanksgiving 3 page 133
Thanksgiving 4 page 136
Thanksgiving 5 page 139
The Great Thanksgiving (Third Order) is found on page 176.

Thanksgiving 1

[The Lord be with you.
And also with you.]

Lift up your hearts.
We lift them to the Lord.

Let us give thanks to the Lord our God.
It is right to give our thanks and praise.

A Seasonal Preface (see pages 147–63) may be substituted for 'All glory and honour ... saying:'

All glory and honour be yours always and everywhere,
mighty Creator, everliving God.

We give you thanks and praise for our Saviour Jesus Christ,
who by the power of your Spirit was born of Mary
and lived as one of us.

By his death on the cross
and rising to new life,
he offered the one true sacrifice for sin
and obtained an eternal deliverance for his people.

Therefore with angels and archangels,
and with all the company of heaven,
we proclaim your great and glorious name,
for ever praising you and saying:

Holy, holy, holy Lord, God of power and might,
Heaven and earth are full of your glory.
Hosanna in the highest.

[**Blessed is he who comes in the name of the Lord.**
Hosanna in the highest.]

Merciful God, we thank you
for these gifts of your creation,
this bread and wine,
and we pray that by your Word and Holy Spirit,
we who eat and drink them
may be partakers of Christ's body and blood.

On the night he was betrayed Jesus took bread;
and when he had given you thanks
he broke it, and gave it to his disciples, saying,

'Take, eat. This is my body given for you.
Do this in remembrance of me.'

After supper, he took the cup,
   and again giving you thanks
   he gave it to his disciples, saying,
   'Drink from this, all of you.
   This is my blood of the new covenant
   shed for you and for many
   for the forgiveness of sins.
   Do this, as often as you drink it, in remembrance of me.'

The memorial acclamation is used here or below.

**Christ has died.
Christ is risen.
Christ will come again.**

Therefore we do as our Saviour has commanded:
   proclaiming his offering of himself
   made once for all upon the cross,
   his mighty resurrection and glorious ascension,
   and looking for his coming again,
   we celebrate, with this bread and this cup,
   his one perfect and sufficient sacrifice
   for the sins of the whole world.

The memorial acclamation may be used here.

Renew us by your Holy Spirit,
   unite us in the body of your Son,
   and bring us with all your people
   into the joy of your eternal kingdom;
   through Jesus Christ our Lord,
   with whom, and in whom,
   in the fellowship of the Holy Spirit,
   we worship you, Father,
   in songs of never-ending praise:

**Blessing and honour and glory and power
are yours for ever and ever. Amen.**

Please turn to page 141.

Thanksgiving 2

[The Lord be with you.
And also with you.]

Lift up your hearts.
We lift them to the Lord.

Let us give thanks to the Lord our God.
It is right to give our thanks and praise.

It is right to praise you, faithful God,
    always and everywhere,
    for with your only begotten Son
    and life-giving Spirit,
    you are the one true God from everlasting to everlasting.

At the dawn of time you wrought from nothing
    a universe of beauty and splendour,
    bringing light from darkness
    and order from chaos.

You formed us, male and female, in your image,
    and endowed us with creative power.

We turned away from you but you did not abandon us.
    You called us by name and searched us out,
    making a covenant of mercy,
    giving the law, and teaching justice by the prophets.

And so we praise you,
    joining with your faithful people of every time and place,
    singing the eternal song:

Holy, holy, holy Lord, God of power and might,
heaven and earth are full of your glory.
Hosanna in the highest.
[**Blessed is he who comes in the name of the Lord.**
Hosanna in the highest.]

When the fullness of time was come,
    you sent your Son to be born of Mary.

Bright image of your glory,
> he learnt obedience to you in all things,
> even to death on a cross,
> breaking the power of evil,
> freeing us from sin, and putting death to flight.

You raised him from death,
> exalting him to glory,
> and the new day dawned.

On the night he was betrayed
> your Son Jesus Christ shared food with his friends,
> his companions on the way.

While at table he took bread,
> blessed, and broke it,
> and giving it to them, said:
> 'Take, eat; this is my body.'

He took a cup of wine,
> and, giving thanks, he gave it to them, and said,
> 'This is my blood of the covenant,
> which is poured out for many.
> Do this in remembrance of me.'

The memorial acclamation is used here or below.

Christ has died.
Christ is risen.
Christ will come again.

Therefore, living God, as we obey his command,
> we remember his life of obedience to you,
> his suffering and death,
> his resurrection and exaltation,
> and his promise to be with us for ever.
> With this bread and this cup
> we celebrate his saving death until he comes.

The memorial acclamation may be used here.

Accept, we pray, our sacrifice of praise and thanksgiving,
> and send your Holy Spirit upon us and our celebration
> that all who eat and drink at this table
> may be strengthened by Christ's body and blood
> to serve you in the world.

As one body and one holy people,
> may we proclaim the everlasting gospel
> of Jesus Christ our Lord,
> through whom, with whom, and in whom,
> in the unity of the Holy Spirit,
> all glory is yours, eternal God, now and for ever.
> **Amen.**

or

**Blessing and honour and glory and power
are yours for ever and ever. Amen.**

Please turn to page 141.

Thanksgiving 3

[The Lord be with you.
And also with you.]

Lift up your hearts.
We lift them to the Lord.

Let us give thanks to the Lord our God.
It is right to give our thanks and praise.

The following Preface is omitted if a Seasonal or other Proper Preface is used.

It is indeed right,
it is our duty, our joy and our salvation,
that we should at all times and in all places
give thanks to you, almighty and everlasting God,
through Jesus Christ your only Son our Lord.

For he is the true high priest,
who has freed us from our sins
and made us a royal priesthood
to serve you, our God and Father.

Therefore with angels and archangels,
and with all the company of heaven,
we proclaim your great and glorious name,
for ever praising you and saying:

**Holy, holy, holy Lord, God of power and might,
Heaven and earth are full of your glory.
Hosanna in the highest.**
**[Blessed is he who comes in the name of the Lord.
Hosanna in the highest.]**

Holy and gracious God,
all creation rightly gives you praise.
All life, all holiness, comes from you
through your Son, Jesus Christ our Lord,
whom you sent to share our human nature,
to live and die as one of us,
to reconcile us to you,
the God and Father of all.

Hear us, merciful Lord;
> through Christ accept our sacrifice of praise;
> and, by the power of your Word and Holy Spirit,
> sanctify this bread and wine,
> that we who share in this holy sacrament
> may be partakers of Christ's body and blood.

Who, when his hour had come,
> on the night before he went up to the cross
> to make full atonement for the sins of the whole world,
> offering once for all his one sacrifice of himself,
> took bread and gave you thanks;
> he broke it and gave it to his disciples, saying,
> 'Take, eat:
> this is my body which is given for you;
> do this in remembrance of me.'

In the same way, after supper
> he took the cup and gave you thanks;
> he gave it to them, saying,
> 'Drink this, all of you;
> this is my blood of the new covenant
> which is shed for you and for many
> for the forgiveness of sins.
> Do this, as often as you drink it,
> in remembrance of me.'

[Let us proclaim the mystery of faith:]
> **Christ has died.**
> **Christ is risen.**
> **Christ will come again.**

Therefore, in obedience to his command,
> we commemorate and celebrate
> his saving passion and death,
> his mighty resurrection and ascension into heaven
> and we eagerly await his coming again in glory.

We thank you that by your grace alone
> you have accepted us in Christ;
> and here we offer you a spiritual sacrifice,
> holy and acceptable in your sight.
> Through Christ, receive this our duty and service,
> and grant that we who eat and drink these holy gifts
> may, by your Holy Spirit,
> be one body in Christ,
> and serve you in unity and peace.

In your grace and mercy,
> bring us to the joy of your eternal kingdom
> with all the company of the redeemed.
> May we praise you in union with them,
> and give you glory through your Son, Jesus Christ.

Through him, with him, in him,
> in the unity of the Holy Spirit,

either

> all glory and honour is yours, gracious Father,
> for ever and ever. **Amen.**

or

> we worship you, Father eternal,
> in songs of never-ending praise:
>
> **Blessing and honour and glory and power
> be yours for ever and ever. Amen.**
>
> *Please turn to page 141.*

Thanksgiving 4

[The Lord be with you.
And also with you.]

Lift up your hearts.
We lift them to the Lord.

Let us give thanks to the Lord our God.
It is right to give our thanks and praise.

All thanks and praise, glory and honour,
be yours at all times, in every place,
holy and loving Father, true and living God.

We praise you that through your eternal Word
you brought the universe into being
and made us in your own image.

You have given us this earth to care for and delight in,
and with its bounty you preserve our life.

We thank you that you bound yourself to the human race
with the promises of a gracious covenant
and called us to serve you in love and peace.

Above all, we give you thanks for your Son,
our Saviour Jesus Christ:
born as one of us, he lived our common life
and offered his life to you in perfect obedience and trust.

By his death he delivered us from sin, brought us new life,
and reconciled us to you and to one another.

Therefore with angels and archangels,
with apostles, and prophets,
with holy men and women of every age,
we proclaim your great and glorious name:

**Holy, holy, holy Lord, God of power and might,
heaven and earth are full of your glory.
Hosanna in the highest.**

**[Blessed is he who comes in the name of the Lord.
Hosanna in the highest.]**

Holy God, we thank you
    for these gifts of your creation, this bread and wine,
    and we pray that we who eat and drink them
    in obedience to our Saviour Christ,
    by the power of the Holy Spirit,
    may be partakers of his body and blood,
    and be made one with him and with each other
    in peace and love.
On the night he was betrayed Jesus took bread;
    and when he had given you thanks
    he broke it, and gave it to his disciples, saying,
    'Take, eat. This is my body given for you.
    Do this in remembrance of me.'
After supper, he took the cup,
    and again giving you thanks
    he gave it to his disciples, saying,
    'Drink from this, all of you.
    This is my blood of the new covenant
    shed for you and for many
    for the forgiveness of sins.
    Do this, as often as you drink it, in remembrance of me.'

The memorial acclamation is used here or below.

**Christ has died.
Christ is risen.
Christ will come again.**

Therefore we do as our Saviour has commanded:
    proclaiming his offering of himself
    made once for all upon the cross,
    his mighty resurrection and glorious ascension,
    and looking for his coming again,
    we celebrate, with this bread and this cup,
    his one perfect and sufficient sacrifice
    for the sins of the whole world.

The memorial acclamation may be used here.

As we eat and drink this holy sacrament,
  renew us by your Spirit
  that we may be united in the body of your Son
  and serve you as a royal priesthood
  in the joy of your eternal kingdom.
Receive our praises, Father,
  through Jesus Christ our Lord,
  with whom and in whom,
  by the power of the Holy Spirit,
  we worship you in songs of never-ending praise:

**Blessing and honour and glory and power
are yours for ever and ever. Amen.**

Please turn to page 141.

Thanksgiving 5

[The Lord be with you.
And also with you.]

Lift up your hearts.
We lift them to the Lord.

Let us give thanks to the Lord our God.
It is right to give our thanks and praise.

Special thanksgivings appropriate for the season or the occasion may be inserted at appropriate places in this prayer.

Loving God,
we thank you for this world of wonder and delight.
You have given it to us to care for,
so that all your creatures may enjoy its bounty.
Lord our God,
we give you thanks and praise.

We thank you that when we turned away from you,
you sent Jesus to live and work as one of us,
and bring us back to you.
He showed us how to love you
and set us free to love and serve one another.
Lord our God,
we give you thanks and praise.

We thank you that on the cross
Jesus took away our sin,
all that keeps us from each other and from you.
He frees us from hate and fear,
from all that destroys love and trust.
Lord our God,
we give you thanks and praise.

And so with everyone who believes in you,
with all the saints and angels,
we rejoice and praise you, saying:

**Holy, holy, holy Lord, God of power and might,
heaven and earth are full of your glory.
Hosanna in the highest.**

And now we thank you
   for these gifts of bread and wine;
   may we who receive them,
   as Jesus said,
   share his body and his blood.
On the night he was betrayed, he took bread
   and gave you thanks.
   He broke the bread and gave it to his friends, and said,
   'Take and eat. This is my body given for you.
   Do this in remembrance of me.'
After supper he took the cup
   and gave you thanks.
   He shared the cup with them and said,
   'This is my blood poured out
   so that sins may be forgiven.
   Do this in remembrance of me.'

The memorial acclamation is used here or below.

**Christ has died.
Christ is risen.
Christ will come again.**

You have gathered us together
   to feed on Christ
   and to remember all he has done for us:

The memorial acclamation may be used here.

Fill us with your Spirit
   that we may follow Jesus
   in all we do and say,
   working for justice and bringing your peace
   to this world that you have made.
Accept our prayers through Jesus Christ our Lord.
   **Blessing and honour and glory and power
   are yours for ever and ever. Amen.**

27 *If the Lord's Prayer has not already been said, it is said here or after the communion. The priest says*

As our Saviour Christ has taught us, we are confident to pray,

Our Father in heaven,
  hallowed be your name,
  your kingdom come,
  your will be done,
    on earth as in heaven.
Give us today our daily bread.
Forgive us our sins
  as we forgive those who sin against us.
Save us from the time of trial
  and deliver us from evil.

For the kingdom, the power, and the glory are yours now and for ever. Amen.

THE BREAKING OF THE BREAD AND THE COMMUNION

28 *The priest breaks the bread. One of the following may be said.*

[We break this bread to share in the body of Christ.]
We who are many are one body,
  for we all share in the one bread.

or

As this broken bread was once many grains,
which have been gathered together and made one bread:
  so may your Church be gathered
  from the ends of the earth into your kingdom.

29 *The priest and other communicants receive the Holy Communion.*

The sacrament is given with the following words.

The body of our Lord Jesus Christ, which was given for you, preserve your body and soul to everlasting life. Take and eat this in remembrance that Christ died for you, and feed on him in your heart by faith with thanksgiving.

and

The blood of our Lord Jesus Christ, which was shed for you, preserve your body and soul to everlasting life. Drink this in remembrance that Christ's blood was shed for you, and be thankful.

or

The priest says

[The gifts of God for the people of God.]
Come let us take this holy sacrament of the body and blood of Christ in remembrance that he died for us, and feed on him in our hearts by faith with thanksgiving.

The sacrament is given with the following words, after which the communicant responds **Amen.**

The body of Christ [the bread of heaven] keep you in eternal life. **Amen.**

The blood of Christ [the cup of salvation] keep you in eternal life. **Amen.**

During the communion, psalms, hymns or anthems such as those on pages 145–46 may be sung or said.

THE SENDING OUT OF GOD'S PEOPLE

30   *The priest says one of the following or another suitable prayer (see the Seasonal Variations, pages 147–63).*

a   Gracious God,
     we thank you that in this sacrament
     you assure us of your goodness and love.
     Accept our sacrifice of praise and thanksgiving
     and help us to grow in love and obedience
     that we may serve you in the world
     and finally be brought to that table
     where all your saints feast with you for ever.

or

b   Bountiful God,
     at this table you graciously feed us
     with the bread of life and the cup of eternal salvation.
     May we who have reached out our hands to receive
        this sacrament
     be strengthened in your service;
     we who have sung your praises
     tell of your glory and truth in our lives;
     we who have seen the greatness of your love
     see you face to face in your kingdom
     and come to worship you with all your saints for ever.

or

c   Living God,
     in this holy meal you fill us with new hope.
     May the power of your love,
     which we have known in word and sacrament,
     continue your saving work among us,
     give us courage for our pilgrimage,
     and bring us to the joys you promise.

or

d   Father of all
     we give you thanks and praise
     that when we were still far off
     you met us in your Son and brought us home.

Dying and living, he declared your love,
gave us grace, and opened the gate of glory.
May we who share Christ's body live his risen life;
we who drink his cup bring life to others;
we whom the Spirit lights give light to the world.
**Keep us in this hope that we have grasped;
so we and all your children shall be free,
and the whole earth live to praise your name.**

If this prayer is said, ¶ 31 may be omitted.

31 *All say together, either*

Father,
**we offer ourselves to you
as a living sacrifice
through Jesus Christ our Lord.
Send us out in the power of your Spirit
to live and work to your praise and glory.**

or

Most loving God,
**you send us into the world you love.
Give us grace to go thankfully and with courage
in the power of your Spirit.**

32 *A hymn may be sung.*

33 *The priest says this or an appropriate seasonal Blessing.*

The peace of God which passes all understanding keep your hearts and minds in the knowledge and love of God, and of his Son, Jesus Christ our Lord;
and the blessing of God almighty, the Father, the Son, and the Holy Spirit, be among you and remain with you always. **Amen**.

34 *The deacon may say*

Go in peace to love and serve the Lord:
In the name of Christ. Amen

or

Go in the peace of Christ.
Thanks be to God.

During the Easter season 'Alleluia, alleluia' may be added to the dismissal and the people's response.

Additional Prayers and Anthems

Confession and Kyrie

The confession (¶6) and Kyrie (¶8) may be replaced by a Litany of Confession using these or other appropriate words. See also page 198.

Lord, we have sinned in thought, word and deed:
  Lord have mercy
    Lord have mercy

We are truly sorry and we ask you to forgive us:
  Christ have mercy
    Christ have mercy

Help us by your Spirit to live in newness of life:
  Lord have mercy
    Lord have mercy

Memorial acclamations

The following or other suitable memorial acclamations may be used.

**We remember his death on the cross.
We proclaim the resurrection to new life.
We await Christ's coming in glory.**

**Dying, you destroyed our death.
Rising, you restored our life.
Christ Jesus, come in glory.**

**When we eat this bread and drink this cup,
we proclaim your death, Lord Jesus,
until you come in glory.**

**Lord, by your cross and resurrection
you have set us free.
You are the Saviour of the world.**

The deacon may introduce the memorial acclamations in these or other suitable words:

In obedience to this command:
In faith we acclaim you, O Christ:
Let us proclaim the mystery of faith:

Invitations to Communion

Either of the following may precede the invitation on page 142.

Jesus is the Lamb of God
who takes away the sins of the world.
Happy are those who are called to his supper.
**Lord, I am not worthy to receive you,
but only say the word, and I shall be healed.**

The gifts of God for the people of God.
**Jesus Christ is holy,
Jesus Christ is Lord,
to the glory of God the Father.**

Anthems

Jesus, Lamb of God, have mercy on us.
Jesus, bearer of our sins, have mercy on us.
Jesus, redeemer of the world, grant us your peace.

Lamb of God, you take away the sin of the world,
have mercy on us.
Lamb of God, you take away the sin of the world,
have mercy on us.
Lamb of God, you take away the sin of the world,
grant us your peace.

The following are especially appropriate during the season of Easter.

Alleluia! Christ our Passover is sacrificed for us;
Therefore let us keep the feast. Alleluia!

The disciples knew the Lord Jesus
in the breaking of the bread.
*The disciples knew the Lord Jesus
in the breaking of the bread.*

The bread which we break, alleluia,
is the communion of the body of Christ.
*The disciples knew the Lord Jesus
in the breaking of the bread.*

We are one body, alleluia,
for though many we share one bread.
*The disciples knew the Lord Jesus
in the breaking of the bread.*

Alternative refrain

Be known to us, Lord Jesus, in the breaking of the bread.

Seasonal Variations

Advent

Invitation to Confession

The Lord comes, bringing to light things now hidden in darkness, and disclosing the purposes of the heart.

Silence may be kept

Let us open our hearts and prepare for his coming, confessing our sins in penitence and faith.

Preface

All glory and honour be yours always and everywhere,
mighty Creator, everliving God.
We give you thanks and praise for your Son,
our Saviour Jesus Christ,
who by the power of your Spirit was born of Mary
and lived as one of us.
By his death on the cross
and rising to new life,
he offered the one true sacrifice for sin
and obtained an eternal deliverance for his people.
We thank you that when he shall come again
in power and great triumph to judge the world,
we may with joy behold his appearing,
and in confidence stand before him
who redeems us from sin and death
and makes us heirs of everlasting life.
Therefore with angels and archangels,
and with all the company of heaven,
we proclaim your great and glorious name,
for ever praising you and saying:

or

All glory and honour be yours always and everywhere,
mighty Creator, everliving God.
We give you thanks and praise for your Son,
our Saviour Jesus Christ,
who was looked for by the prophets,
heralded by the Baptist
announced by an angel,
born of the Virgin Mary,
and revealed at last to men and women of every race.
By his death on the cross
and rising to new life,
he offered the one true sacrifice for sin
and obtained an eternal deliverance for his people.
Therefore with angels and archangels,
and with all the company of heaven,
we proclaim your great and glorious name,
for ever praising you and saying:

Prayer after Communion

God for whom we wait,
we thank you that you have fed us with the bread of life
and the cup of salvation.
As we joyfully await your Son,
keep us ever watchful
that we may be ready to stand before him
on the day of his coming.

Blessing

Christ the Sun of Righteousness shine upon you,
and make you ready to meet him when he comes in glory;
and the blessing...

Christmas

Invitation to Confession

Christ the grace of God has dawned upon the world with healing for all.

Silence may be kept.

Let us bring our weaknesses and infirmities to him, confessing our sins in penitence and faith.

Preface

All glory and honour be yours always and everywhere,
mighty Creator, everliving God.
We give you thanks and praise for your Son,
our Saviour Jesus Christ,
who by the power of your Spirit was born of Mary
and lived as one of us.
In your Word made flesh
you have caused a new light to shine in our hearts,
to give knowledge of your glory
in the face of Jesus Christ.
By his death on the cross
and rising to new life,
he offered the one true sacrifice for sin
and obtained an eternal deliverance for his people.
Therefore with angels and archangels,
and with all the company of heaven,
we proclaim your great and glorious name,
for ever praising you and saying:

Prayer after Communion

God of heaven, dwelling among us,
we thank you for feeding us with this holy food.
By your grace keep us ever faithful
to your Word made flesh
that as his body in the world
we may bring your presence to all people.

Blessing

Christ the Son of God, born of Mary, fill you with his grace to trust his promises and obey his will;
and the blessing…

Epiphany

Invitation to Confession

Christ the Son of God has been revealed as a light to the nations.

Silence may be kept.

Let us bring our darkness to his light, confessing our sins in penitence and faith.

Preface

All glory and honour be yours always and everywhere,
mighty Creator, everliving God.
We give you thanks and praise for your Son,
our Saviour Jesus Christ,
who by the power of your Spirit was born of Mary
and lived as one of us.
You anointed him as Messiah,
the light of the nations,
and revealed him as the hope
of all who thirst for righteousness and peace.
By his death on the cross
and rising to new life,
he offered the one true sacrifice for sin
and obtained an eternal deliverance for his people.
Therefore with angels and archangels,
and with all the company of heaven,
we proclaim your great and glorious name,
for ever praising you and saying:

Prayer after Communion

God of the nations,
we thank you for nourishing us with this holy sacrament.
Guide us by your presence,
that we may bring your light to those who dwell in darkness,
and establish your justice in the earth.

Blessing

May Christ the Son of God be manifest to you,
that your lives may be a light to the world;
and the blessing…

Ash Wednesday and Lent

Invitation to Confession

Compassion and forgiveness belong to the Lord our God, though we have rebelled and wandered far off.

Silence may be kept.

Let us then ask for mercy, confessing our sins in penitence and faith.

Preface

All glory and honour be yours always and everywhere,
mighty Creator, everliving God.
We give you thanks and praise for your Son,
our Saviour Jesus Christ,
who by the power of your Spirit was born of Mary
and lived as one of us.
He was tempted in every way as we are,
yet he did not sin.
By his death on the cross
and rising to new life,
he offered the one true sacrifice for sin
and obtained an eternal deliverance for his people.
By his grace we are able
to triumph over every evil,
and to walk in the way of his love.
Therefore with angels and archangels,
and with all the company of heaven,
we proclaim your great and glorious name,
for ever praising you and saying:

Prayer after Communion

God of mercy,
may we who have shared in this holy meal
know your forgiveness in our lives,
bring your reconciliation to others,
and be a sign of your wholeness in this broken world.

or

Compassionate and loving God,
through your Son Jesus Christ you have fed us
and have reconciled your people to yourself.
Following his example of fasting and prayer,
may we obey you with willing hearts
and serve one another in holy love.

Blessing

> Christ our Saviour draw you to himself,
> that you may find in him crucified
> a sure ground for faith,
> a firm support for hope,
> and the assurance of sin forgiven
> [and the blessing…]

or

> Grant, merciful Lord,
> to your faithful people pardon and peace,
> that they may be cleansed from all their sins
> and serve you with a quiet mind;
> through Christ our Lord.

During Lent, 'and the blessing…' may be omitted.

Holy Week

Invitation to Confession

> God shows great love for us in that while we were still sinners Christ died for us.
>
> *Silence may be kept.*
>
> Let us then confess our sins in penitence and faith.

Preface

Holy Week

> All glory and honour be yours always and everywhere,
> mighty Creator, everliving God.
> We give you thanks and praise for your Son,
> our Saviour Jesus Christ,
> who became obedient unto death, even death on a cross.
> He offered the one true sacrifice for sin,
> and obtained an eternal deliverance for his people.
> The tree of defeat became the tree of victory;
> where life was lost, there life has been restored.
> Therefore with angels and archangels,
> and with all the company of heaven,
> we proclaim your great and glorious name,
> for ever praising you and saying:

Maundy Thursday

All glory and honour be yours always and everywhere,
mighty Creator, everliving God.
We give you thanks and praise for your Son,
our Saviour Jesus Christ,
who became obedient unto death, even death on a cross.
He offered the one true sacrifice for sin,
and obtained an eternal deliverance for his people.
When his hour had come, in his great love
he gave this supper to his disciples,
that we might proclaim his death,
and feast with him in his kingdom.
Therefore with angels and archangels,
and with all the company of heaven,
we proclaim your great and glorious name,
for ever praising you and saying:

Prayer after Communion

Holy Week

God our help and strength,
through these holy mysteries
confirm our faith
that by the death and resurrection of your Son
we may walk in the way of salvation.

Maundy Thursday

Holy God, source of all love,
on this night of betrayal
Jesus commanded his disciples
to love one another as he loved them.
We thank you for feeding us in this supper.
Give us the will to serve others
as he was servant of all.

Good Friday

Most merciful God,
you have restored us to life
by the triumphant death of Jesus, your Son.
Continue his healing work within us
that all who partake in this communion
may give themselves wholly to your service.

Easter
Invitation to Confession

Christ our Passover Lamb has been offered for us, therefore we come to celebrate the festival.

Silence may be kept.

Let us confess our sins in penitence and faith, with a sincere and a true heart.

Preface

All glory and honour be yours always and everywhere,
mighty Creator, everliving God.
We give you thanks and praise for your Son,
our Saviour Jesus Christ,
who by the power of your Spirit was born of Mary
and lived as one of us.
By his death on the cross,
he offered the one true sacrifice for sin,
and obtained an eternal deliverance for his people.
And now we give you thanks
that you raised him to life triumphant,
and exalted him in glory.
By his victory over death,
the reign of sin is ended,
a new day has dawned,
a broken world is restored
and we are made whole once more.
Therefore with angels and archangels,
and with all the company of heaven,
we proclaim your great and glorious name,
for ever praising you and saying:

or

All glory and honour be yours always and everywhere,
mighty Creator, everliving God.
We give you thanks and praise for your Son,
our Saviour Jesus Christ,
who by the power of your Spirit was born of Mary
and lived as one of us.
He is the true Paschal Lamb
who was offered for us
and has taken away the sin of the world.
And now we give you thanks

that you raised him in triumph from the dead.
By his death, he has destroyed death
and by his rising to life again
has restored us to eternal life.
Therefore with angels and archangels,
and with all the company of heaven,
we proclaim your great and glorious name,
for ever praising you and saying:

Prayer after Communion

Eternal God, giver of life,
in the breaking of the bread we know the risen Lord.
May we who celebrate this holy feast
walk in his risen light
and bring new life to all creation.

or

Most glorious Lord of life,
we thank you that you nourish us
in these Easter mysteries.
Fill us with the Spirit of love
and unite us in faith,
that we may witness to the resurrection
and show your glory to all the world.

Blessing

The God of peace, who brought again from the dead our Lord Jesus, the great shepherd of the sheep, through the blood of the everlasting covenant, make you perfect in every good work to do his will, working in you what is pleasing in his sight;
and the blessing…

or

Almighty God,
who redeemed us through the resurrection of Christ,
[who raised us to newness of life through the waters of baptism,]
and has brought us out of slavery into everlasting freedom,
give you joy and peace in faith and bring you to your eternal inheritance;
and the blessing…

Ascension

Invitation to Confession

Christ has entered heaven itself, there to appear before God on our behalf.

Silence may be kept.

Let us therefore draw near in full assurance of faith, and confess our sins to the God of grace.

Preface

All glory and honour be yours always and everywhere,
mighty Creator, everliving God.
We give you thanks and praise for your Son,
our Saviour Jesus Christ,
who by the power of your Spirit was born of Mary
and lived as one of us.
By his death on the cross
and rising to new life,
he offered the one true sacrifice for sin
and obtained an eternal deliverance for his people.
You have highly exalted him,
and given him the name which is above all other names,
that at the name of Jesus every knee should bow
and every tongue confess that Jesus Christ is Lord.
Therefore with angels and archangels,
and with all the company of heaven,
we proclaim your great and glorious name,
for ever praising you and saying:

Prayer after Communion

God of glory
you sent your Son Jesus Christ into the world
to preach the gospel of the kingdom.
Strengthen us who share this meal to continue his mission
by living the good news we proclaim.

Blessing

Christ our exalted king pour upon you his abundant gifts and bring you to reign with him in glory;
and the blessing…

Day of Pentecost

Invitation to Confession

The Spirit of truth comes to convict of sin, of righteousness, and of judgement.

Silence may be kept.

Let us then open our hearts and confess our sins in penitence and faith.

Preface

All glory and honour be yours always and everywhere,
mighty Creator, everliving God.
We give you thanks and praise for your Son,
our Saviour Jesus Christ,
who by the power of your Spirit was born of Mary
and lived as one of us.
By his death on the cross
and rising to new life,
he offered the one true sacrifice for sin
and obtained an eternal deliverance for his people.
Today we give you thanks that
in fulfilment of your promise
you pour forth your Spirit upon us,
filling us with gifts and leading us into all truth.
You give us power to proclaim your gospel to all nations
and to serve you as a royal priesthood.
Therefore with angels and archangels,
and with all the company of heaven,
we proclaim your great and glorious name,
for ever praising you and saying:

Prayer after Communion

Giver of life and love,
we thank you that in this heavenly banquet
you invigorate and renew us.
Living in the unity of the Spirit,
may we boldly use your gifts
to continue your work in the world.

Blessing

May the Spirit lead you into all truth,
giving you grace to confess that Jesus Christ is Lord,
and to proclaim the wonderful works of God;
and the blessing…

or

God stir up within you the gift of the Spirit
that you may confess Jesus Christ as Lord and proclaim the joy of the
everlasting gospel wherever you may be;
and the blessing…

Trinity Sunday: First Sunday after Pentecost
Invitation to Confession

'Hear, O Israel, the Lord our God, the Lord is one; you shall love the Lord your God with all your heart, and with all your soul, and with all your mind, and with all your strength.' Jesus said: 'This is the great and first commandment. And a second is like it: you shall love your neighbour as yourself.'

Silence may be kept.

Let us therefore bring our sins before the one true God, in penitence and faith.

Preface

All glory and honour be yours always and everywhere,
mighty Creator, everliving God.
We give you thanks and praise for your Son,
our Saviour Jesus Christ,
who by the power of your Spirit was born of Mary
and lived as one of us.
By his death on the cross
and rising to new life,
he offered the one true sacrifice for sin
and obtained an eternal deliverance for his people.
Through him, you have revealed to us your glory
in the community of your love,
three persons, one God,
ever to be worshipped and adored.
Therefore with angels and archangels,
and with all the company of heaven,
we proclaim your great and glorious name,
for ever praising you and saying:

Prayer after Communion

Almighty and eternal God,
may we who have received this sacrament
of your Son's body and blood
worship you in all we do,
proclaim your word to all the world,
and live in the power of your Spirit.

Blessing

God the Holy Trinity make you strong in faith and love,
defend you on every side,
and guide you in all truth and peace;
and the blessing...

Saints

Invitation to Confession

We are surrounded by a great cloud of witnesses.

Silence may be kept.

Let us then run our race, laying aside every weight and bringing our sins to the Lord in penitence and faith.

Preface

All glory and honour be yours always and everywhere,
mighty Creator, everliving God.
We give you thanks and praise for your Son,
our Saviour Jesus Christ,
who by the power of your Spirit was born of Mary
and lived as one of us.
By his death on the cross
and rising to new life,
he offered the one true sacrifice for sin
and obtained an eternal deliverance for his people.
And now we give you thanks because
you have called us into the fellowship of [N and]
all your saints,
and set before us the example of their witness
and the fruit of your Spirit in their lives.
Therefore with angels and archangels,
and with all the company of heaven,
we proclaim your great and glorious name,
for ever praising you and saying:

Prayer after Communion

God, the source of all holiness:
may we who have shared at this table
as strangers and pilgrims on earth
be welcomed with [N and] all your saints
to the heavenly feast in your kingdom.

Blessing

God give you grace to follow [N and] all the saints in faith and hope and love;
and the blessing…

The Blessed Virgin Mary

Invitation to Confession

The Lord has mercy on those who fear him from generation to generation.

Silence may be kept.

Let us humbly confess our sins in penitence and faith, confident that God will raise us up.

Preface

A Preface for Christmas or the following:

All glory and honour be yours always and everywhere,
mighty Creator, everliving God.
We give you thanks and praise for your Son,
our Saviour Jesus Christ,
who was born and lived as one of us.
By his death on the cross
and rising to new life,
he offered the one true sacrifice for sin
and obtained an eternal deliverance for his people.
And now we give you thanks for the obedience
of your servant Mary,
who by your grace answered your call
to be the mother of your Son.
With all generations we call her blessed,
and with her we rejoice in the greatness of your salvation.
Therefore with angels and archangels,
and with all the company of heaven,
we proclaim your great and glorious name,
for ever praising you and saying:

Prayer after Communion

God our Saviour,
your word proclaims our salvation
which we taste in the bread of life.
Grant us the humble obedience we see in Mary
that we, too, may respond as willing servants
and bear your Word to our world.

Blessing

Christ the Son of God, born of Mary, gladden our hearts by his coming to dwell among us, and fill us with joy and peace; and the blessing…

Australia

The invitation to confession is especially suitable for services whose theme is reconciliation between the indigenous and non-indigenous peoples of Australia.

Invitation to Confession

If my people who are called by my name humble themselves, pray, seek my face, and turn from their wicked ways, then I will hear from heaven, and will forgive their sin and heal their land.

2 Chronicles 7.14

Though Christ has called us into one body, the oneness of the peoples of this land has been broken by acts of oppression and the failure of compassion.

Silence may be kept.

Let us therefore confess our brokenness, confident in God's power and promise to make us whole.

The general confession and absolution on page 126 or the litany of confession on page 199 or other suitable prayers may be used.

Preface

All glory and honour, thanks and praise,
be yours now and always,
Lord of every time and place,
God beyond our dreaming.
We give you thanks that from the beginning of time,
your Spirit has brooded over this ancient land.
In the fullness of time you revealed your Son,
our Saviour Jesus Christ,
who by the power of your Spirit was born of Mary
and lived as one of us.
By his death on the cross
and rising to new life,
he offered the one true sacrifice for sin,
and obtained an eternal deliverance for his people.
We give you thanks that in him
you have revealed to us your presence
in the vastness of this land,
your love in its fruitfulness, and
your purpose in its cycles of death and renewed life.

Therefore with angels and archangels,
and with all the company of heaven,
we proclaim your great and glorious name,
for ever praising you and saying:

Prayer after Communion

Heavenly Father, you have created all humanity
in your image and likeness,
and have revealed your plan and purpose
in calling us your friends and family.
As we have shared this holy meal,
inspire our hearts to see
every man, woman and child
given the dignity and value
which is your purpose and your gift;
through Jesus Christ our Lord.

The Lent post-communion prayer is also suitable.

Blessing

God of this ancient land, through baptism you have given us an inheritance into one family, give us grace to walk together in the unity of Christ Jesus;
and the blessing…

Ordination

Preface

Blessed are you, gracious God,
creator of heaven and earth.
We give you thanks and praise
for your Son our Saviour Jesus Christ.
Who came not to be served, but to serve,
and to give his life as a ransom for many.
He taught your word with boldness,
and offered himself to you in perfect obedience.
He cared for all as the good shepherd,
and laid down his life for his sheep.
By his death and rising to new life
he brought new life to your people.
In baptism you have united us to him,
and brought us out of darkness to light.

And now we give you thanks that
in fulfilment of your promise
you pour out your Spirit upon us,
filling us with your gifts and leading us into all truth.
You give us power to proclaim your gospel to all nations,
and to serve you as a royal priesthood.

For deacons.

You call out those who will serve you as deacons,
and commission them for the service of others,
that the pattern of Christ's rule may be seen among us.

For priests and bishops.

You ordain ministers to proclaim your word,
to care for your people,
and to celebrate the sacraments of the new covenant.

Therefore, with them, and with all your saints
who have served you in every age,
we give thanks and lift our voices
to proclaim the glory of your name.

Prayer after Communion

Gracious God,
we thank you for feeding us with the body and blood of your Son,
and for uniting us through him in the fellowship
   of your Holy Spirit.
We thank you for raising up faithful servants
for the ministry of your word and sacraments.
May they be godly examples in word and action,
in love and patience, and in holiness of life,
that *they* may faithfully fulfil *their* ministry.
May your word spoken through them never fail.
Make us, with them, faithful witnesses of the Lord Jesus
   and his resurrection,
that at his coming we may go out with great joy to meet him,
and be found worthy to worship you with all your saints for ever.

Notes

1. For the communion, the Holy Table is spread with a white cloth.
2. In addition to its position at ¶ 1 or ¶ 3, a seasonal sentence may be used after the distribution of holy communion.
3. A deacon or other minister may lead the acclamations at ¶ 2.
4. It is suggested that the *Gloria* or some other hymn of praise be used at ¶ 9 on Sundays (except during Advent and Lent), the weekdays of the Easter season, and on Holy Days. The *Trisagion* is particularly appropriate during Advent and Lent.
5. It is desirable that the readings be read from a prominent lectern or pulpit, and that the gospel be read from either the same place or in the midst of the people. It is recommended that all readings be read from a book or books of appropriate size and dignity.
6. The first and second reading may be introduced by the reader in this way: 'A reading from [the book]…[chapter…beginning at verse…]. One of these readings may be omitted.
7. The use of the psalm in the Ministry of the Word is encouraged (as is singing it). The *Gloria Patri* is best omitted when a psalm is used in this context.
8. The sermon is integral to the Ministry of the Word. A sermon should normally be preached on Sundays and Holy Days.
9. A time of children's ministry may take place at any point during the Ministry of the Word.
10. Silence is important in this rite. It may be observed as follows: before the collect, after any of the readings and/or the sermon, before the confession, after the distribution of the holy communion.
11. At the Greeting of Peace all present may greet one another with a handshake or other suitable sign of reconciliation.
12. When a certain posture is particularly appropriate, it is indicated. Otherwise local custom may be followed. The Great Thanksgiving prayer is a single prayer. Its unity may be obscured by changes in posture in the course of it; standing for the whole of the prayer is recommended.
13. The symbolism of one bread and one cup has great value. It is suggested that one loaf of bread and one chalice of wine only be placed on the table for the Great Thanksgiving. If need be, extra loaves of bread and some suitable jug or other container of wine may also be placed on the table. Other chalices may then be filled from the jug after the Breaking of the Bread. It is sufficient that the bread be that normally eaten and that the wine be fermented juice of the grape.

14 In the Great Thanksgiving prayer, it is customary during the narrative of the Last Supper (commonly called the Words of Institution) for the priest to take hold of the bread during the words concerning the bread, and likewise the cup.

15 At the Breaking of the Bread, the bread should be broken in the sight of all.

16 Any remaining consecrated bread and wine is to be reverently consumed after the distribution of communion or immediately after the service. This may be done at the Holy Table or at a credence table, in a chapel or at some other discreet place.

17 If notices are to be given, they may be given before the prayers, after the Greeting of Peace, before the final blessing, or at another appropriate time.

The Holy Communion
THIRD ORDER

GATHERING IN GOD'S NAME

1   *The priest greets the people. The service may begin with songs or hymns of praise and thanksgiving.*

2   *The minister says this or another suitable Sentence of Scripture.*

Our Lord Jesus Christ said:
You shall love the Lord your God with all your heart, and with all your soul, and with all your mind, and with all your strength. This is the great and first commandment. And a second is like it: You shall love your neighbour as yourself. On these two commandments hang all the law and the prophets.

Matthew 22.37–40, Mark 12.30–31

Let us pray.
**Almighty God,
to whom all hearts are open,
all desires known,
and from whom no secrets are hidden:
cleanse the thoughts of our hearts
by the inspiration of your Holy Spirit,
that we may perfectly love you,
and worthily magnify your holy name,
through Christ our Lord. Amen.**

3   *'Glory to God in the Highest' (page 179) or some other hymn of praise may be sung.*

4   *The Collect of the Day*

THE MINISTRY OF THE WORD

5 *The Bible readings follow, one from the Old Testament and one or two from the New Testament. A reading from the Gospels is always included.*

After each reading the reader may say

Hear the word of the Lord,
thanks be to God.

6 *A psalm or portion of a psalm may be sung or said and a suitable hymn or song may follow any of the readings.*

7 *All stand for the Gospel reading.*

The reader may say

The Gospel of our Lord Jesus Christ according to...
[chapter... verse...]
Glory to you Lord Jesus Christ.

After the Gospel, the reader says

This is the Gospel of the Lord,
or [For] the Gospel of the Lord,
praise to you Lord Jesus Christ.

8 *The Sermon is preached here or after the creed.*

9   *On Sundays the Nicene Creed or the Apostles' Creed is said or sung, all standing.*

We believe in one God,
 the Father, the almighty,
 maker of heaven and earth,
 of all that is, seen and unseen.
We believe in one Lord, Jesus Christ,
 the only Son of God,
 eternally begotten of the Father,
 God from God, Light from Light,
 true God from true God,
 begotten, not made,
 of one being with the Father;
 through him all things were made.
 For us and for our salvation
 he came down from heaven,
 was incarnate of the Holy Spirit and the virgin Mary
 and became truly human.
 For our sake he was crucified under Pontius Pilate;
 he suffered death and was buried.
 On the third day he rose again
 in accordance with the Scriptures;
 he ascended into heaven
 and is seated at the right hand of the Father.
 He will come again in glory to judge
  the living and the dead
 and his kingdom will have no end.
We believe in the Holy Spirit, the Lord, the giver of life,
 who proceeds from the Father and the Son,
 who with the Father and the Son
 is worshipped and glorified,
 who has spoken through the prophets.
 We believe in one holy catholic and apostolic Church.
 We acknowledge one baptism for the forgiveness of sins.
 We look for the resurrection of the dead,
 and the life of the world to come. Amen.

or

> I believe in God, the Father almighty,
>   creator of heaven and earth.
> I believe in Jesus Christ, God's only Son, our Lord,
>   who was conceived by the Holy Spirit,
>   born of the virgin Mary,
>   suffered under Pontius Pilate,
>   was crucified, died, and was buried;
>   he descended to the dead.
>   On the third day he rose from the dead;
>   he ascended into heaven,
>   and is seated at the right hand of the Father;
>   from there he will come to judge
>   the living and the dead.
> I believe in the Holy Spirit,
>   the holy catholic Church,
>   the communion of saints,
>   the forgiveness of sins,
>   the resurrection of the body,
>   and the life everlasting. Amen.

10   *The Sermon is preached here if it has not been preached earlier.*

11   *A hymn or song may follow.*

THE PRAYERS OF THE PEOPLE

12 *One or more members of the congregation may pray, using this form or a suitable alternative (see pages 183–87).*

Almighty God, your Son Jesus Christ has promised that you will hear us when we ask in faith: receive the prayers we offer.

For the nations

We give thanks for... We pray for...

Guide with your wisdom and power the leaders of the nations, so that everyone may live in peace and mutual trust, sharing with justice the resources of the earth. Give the people of this land a spirit of unselfishness, compassion, and fairness in public and private life.

>Father, hear our prayer
>**through Jesus Christ our Lord.**

or

>Lord, in your mercy
>**hear our prayer.**

For the Church

We give thanks for... We pray for...

Send out the light and truth of your gospel and bring people everywhere to know and love you. Enable those who minister among us to commend your truth by their example and teaching. May we gladly receive and obey your word.

>Father, hear our prayer
>**through Jesus Christ our Lord.**

or

>Lord, in your mercy
>**hear our prayer.**

For those in need

We give thanks for... We pray for...

We commend to your fatherly care, merciful God, all who are in sorrow, sickness, discouragement or any other trouble. Give them patience and a firm trust in your goodness. Help those who care for them, and bring us all into the joy of your salvation.

> Father, hear our prayer
> **through Jesus Christ our Lord.**

or

> Lord, in your mercy
> **hear our prayer.**

Thanksgiving for the faithful departed

We give thanks for the life and work of...

We praise you for all your servants whose lives have honoured Christ. Encourage us by their example, so that we may run with perseverance the race that lies before us, and share with them the fullness of joy in your kingdom.

The prayers conclude with

Hear us, Father,
through Jesus Christ our Lord,
> **who lives and reigns with you
> in the unity of the Holy Spirit,
> one God, now and for ever. Amen.**

or

Accept our prayers through Jesus Christ our Lord, who taught us to pray,
**Our Father in heaven,
> hallowed be your name,
> your kingdom come,
> your will be done,
>> on earth as in heaven.
> Give us today our daily bread.
> Forgive us our sins
>> as we forgive those who sin against us.
> Save us from the time of trial
>> and deliver us from evil.
> For the kingdom, the power, and the glory are yours
> now and for ever. Amen.**

PREPARATION FOR THE LORD'S SUPPER

13 *An exhortation may be read (see page 108). One of the following or a suitable alternative may be read.*

As often as you eat this bread and drink the cup, you proclaim the Lord's death until he comes. Whoever, therefore, eats the bread and drinks the cup of the Lord in an unworthy manner will be answerable for the body and blood of the Lord. Examine yourselves, and only then eat of the bread and drink of the cup.

1 Corinthians 11.26–28

Seek the Lord while he may be found, call upon him while he is near; let the wicked forsake their way, and the unrighteous their thoughts; let them return to the Lord, that he may have mercy on them, and to our God, for he will abundantly pardon. For my thoughts are not your thoughts, nor are your ways my ways, says the Lord.

Isaiah 55.6–8

We are God's children now, and what we will be has not yet been made known. But we know that when he appears we shall be like him, for we shall see him as he is. All who have this hope in him purify themselves, just as he is pure.

1 John 3.2–3

14 *A time of silence may follow.*

The deacon or other minister says

Knowing the goodness of God and our failure to respond with love and obedience, let us confess our sins, saying together,

Heavenly Father,
you have loved us with an everlasting love,
but we have broken your holy laws
and have left undone what we ought to have done.
We are sorry for our sins
  and turn away from them.
For the sake of your Son who died for us,
  forgive us, cleanse us and change us.

**By your Holy Spirit,
enable us to live for you;
through Jesus Christ our Lord. Amen.**

15 *The priest stands and declares God's forgiveness in these or other authorised words.*

God is slow to anger and full of compassion,
forgiving all who humbly repent
   and trust in his Son as Saviour and Lord.
God therefore forgives you in Christ Jesus,
in whom there is no condemnation. **Amen.**

One or more of the following passages may also be read as an assurance of God's forgiveness.

God so loved the world that he gave his only Son, so that everyone who believes in him may not perish but may have eternal life.

John 3.16

As far as the east is from the west, so far has God removed our sins from us.

Psalm 103.12

Our Lord Jesus Christ himself bore our sins in his body on the cross, so that we might die to sin and live for righteousness; by his wounds you have been healed.

1 Peter 2.24

THE GREETING OF PEACE

16 *All stand. The Greeting of Peace is introduced with these or other suitable words.*

We are the body of Christ.
His Spirit is with us.

The priest says

The peace of the Lord be always with you.
And also with you.

All may exchange a sign of peace.

17 *The gifts of the people are brought to the Lord's Table. A hymn or song may be sung.*

THE GREAT THANKSGIVING

18 *Bread and the wine for the communion are placed on the Lord's Table. The priest says the following or another authorised Prayer of Thanksgiving and Consecration.*

[The Lord be with you.
And also with you.]
Lift up your hearts.
We lift them to the Lord.
Let us give thanks to the Lord our God.
It is right to give our thanks and praise.

You are worthy, our Lord and God,
  to receive glory and honour and power,
  for you created all things,
  making us in your own image.
We praise you for your Son,
  our Saviour Jesus Christ,
  who by his death on the cross
  and rising to new life
  offered the one true sacrifice for sin
  and obtained an eternal deliverance for his people.
Therefore, we lift our voices to praise you, saying,

**Holy, holy, holy Lord, God of power and might,
heaven and earth are full of your glory.
Hosanna in the highest.**

And now, gracious God, we thank you
  for these gifts of bread and wine,
  and pray that we who receive them,
  in the fellowship of the Holy Spirit,
  according to our Saviour's word,
  in remembrance of his suffering and death,
  may share his body and blood.

On the night before he died, Jesus took bread,
   and when he had given you thanks
   he broke it, and gave it to his disciples, saying,
   'Take and eat. This is my body which is given for you.
   Do this in remembrance of me.'

[If the bread is broken here, the priest may say
We who are many are one body in Christ,
   for we all share in the one bread.]

After supper, he took the cup,
   and again giving you thanks
   he gave it to his disciples, saying,
   'Drink from this, all of you.
   This is my blood of the new covenant
   which is shed for you and for many
   for the forgiveness of sins.
   Do this, as often as you drink it, in remembrance of me.'
We eat this bread and drink this cup
   to proclaim the death of the Lord.
We do this until he returns.
   Come, Lord Jesus!

Father, as we recall his saving death and glorious resurrection,
   may we who share these gifts
   be renewed by your Holy Spirit
   and united in the body of your Son.
Bring us with all your people
   into the joy of your eternal kingdom,
   there to feast at your table and
   join in your eternal praise:

   Worthy is the Lamb, who was slain,
   to receive praise and honour
   and glory and power
   for ever and ever. Amen.

THE BREAKING OF THE BREAD AND THE COMMUNION

19   If the bread has not already been broken, the priest does so here. This may be done in silence, or the following may be said.

[We break this bread to share in the body of Christ.]
We who are many are one body,
for we all share in the one bread.

20   Those who distribute the bread and deliver the cup may say

The body of our Lord Jesus Christ, which was given for you, preserve your body and soul to everlasting life. Take and eat this in remembrance that Christ died for you, and feed on him in your heart by faith with thanksgiving.

The blood of our Lord Jesus Christ, which was shed for you, preserve your body and soul to everlasting life. Drink this in remembrance that Christ's blood was shed for you, and be thankful.

or

The priest may say

Draw near with faith, to feed on Christ in your hearts with thanksgiving.

Those who distribute the bread and deliver the cup may say

The body of Christ keep you in eternal life. **Amen.**
The blood of Christ keep you in eternal life. **Amen.**

THE SENDING OUT OF GOD'S PEOPLE

21 *If the Lord's Prayer has not been said earlier (at ¶ 12), it is said here. This or another thanksgiving is then said.*

Gracious God, thank you for feeding us
with the spiritual food of the body and blood
   of our Saviour Jesus Christ.
Thank you for assuring us of your goodness and love,
and that we are living members of Christ's body.

22 *All say together*

Father,
**we offer ourselves to you
as a living sacrifice
through Jesus Christ our Lord.
Send us out in the power of your Spirit
to live and work to your praise and glory.**

23 *This Hymn of Praise or a suitable alternative may be said or sung.*

**Glory to God in the highest,
and peace to God's people on earth.
Lord God, heavenly King,
almighty God and Father,
   we worship you, we give you thanks,
   we praise you for your glory.**

**Lord Jesus Christ, only Son of the Father,
   Lord God, Lamb of God,
   you take away the sin of the world:
      have mercy on us;
   you are seated at the right hand of the Father:
      receive our prayer.**

**For you alone are the Holy One,
   you alone are the Lord,
   you alone are the Most High
      Jesus Christ,
      with the Holy Spirit,
      in the glory of God the Father. Amen.**

24 *The priest says this or an appropriate seasonal Blessing.*

The peace of God which passes all understanding keep your hearts and minds in the knowledge and love of God, and of his Son, Jesus Christ our Lord;
and the blessing of God almighty, the Father, the Son, and the Holy Spirit, be among you and remain with you always.
Amen.

25 *The deacon may say*

Go in peace to love and serve the Lord:
In the name of Christ. Amen.

Holy Communion

OUTLINE ORDER

This order requires careful preparation by the participants. It is not primarily for use at the principal Sunday celebration.

GATHERING IN GOD'S NAME

There may be singing, an introduction and greeting, scripture sentence and opening prayer.

The 'Gathering' ends with the Collect-the prayer for the day-which also introduces the themes of 'The Ministry of the Word'.

THE MINISTRY OF THE WORD

Two or three Bible readings, one of which is from the Gospel: psalms or songs. On Sundays, it is appropriate to use the Creed.

THE PRAYERS OF THE PEOPLE

The prayers of intercession and thanksgiving may in any suitable form.

CONFESSION AND ABSOLUTION

A confession of sins and absolution is used, especially on Sundays and other Holy Days, as a response to the word of God and in preparation for the celebration of Holy Communion. It may be included as part of *The Gathering of the People'

THE GREETING OF PEACE

PREPARATION OF THE LORD'S TABLE

Some of those present prepare the table: the bread and cup of wine are placed on it.

THE GREAT THANKSGIVING

Priest offers thanksgiving using authorised prayer.

THE BREAKING OF BREAD AND COMMUNION

The breaking of the bread may be done in silence or using suitable words such as ¶28 of the Holy Communion, Second Order.

The priest invites the people to receive communion. Each communicant replies **Amen** to the words of distribution.

THE SENDING OUT OF GOD'S PEOPLE

Suitable post-communion prayers, blessing and dismissal are used.

Acknowledgements

Thanksgiving 3 had its origins in a prayer from the Province of the West Indies, but was freely adapted by the General Synod of the Anglican Church of Australia, 1995.

The prayers after communion for Advent, Ash Wednesday and Lent (second alternative), Holy Week, Maundy Thursday, Good Friday, Easter, Ascension and the Blessed Virgin Mary; the proper prefaces for Incarnation and Pentecost; and the invitation to confession on page 126 are based on *The Book of Alternative Services* of the Anglican Church of Canada, copyright © 1985 by the General Synod of the Anglican Church of Canada. Used with permission.

The proper prefaces for Easter and the Blessed Virgin Mary are from *A New Zealand Prayer Book, He Karakia Mihinare o Aotearoa* © 1989 by the Church of the Province of New Zealand, and used by permission.

The invitations to confession for Advent, Incarnation, Epiphany, Ash Wednesday and Lent, Easter, and Saints are from David Silk, *In Penitence and Faith*, Mowbray, Oxford. © Cassell PLC, London. Used by permission.

The proper preface for Advent (first alternative); the blessings for Ash Wednesday and Lent (second alternative), Easter (second alternative), Pentecost, and Trinity are based on *The Book of Common Prayer* according to the use of The Episcopal Church, Church Hymnal Corporation 1979.

The proper prefaces for Holy Week and Ascension, and the blessing for Advent are from, and the Maundy Thursday preface is based on, *The Alternative Service Book* 1980. Copyright © The Central Board of Finance of the Church of England 1980. Used by permission.

The proper prefaces for Advent (second alternative) and for Epiphany, and the prayer after communion for Saints are from *The Promise of His Glory* 1991. Text © The Central Board of Finance of the Church of England 1990, 1991. Used by permission.

Prayer *d* on p. 143 is by David L. Frost © The Central Board of Finance of the Church of England. Used by permission.

The second prayer on p. 144 is based on a text by the Revd Dr Elizabeth Smith.

The seasonal variations for Australia (p. 161) are based on texts by the Koori Commission of the Anglican Diocese of Canberra and Goulburn.

www.ingramcontent.com/pod-product-compliance
Lightning Source LLC
Chambersburg PA
CBHW071025080526
44587CB00015B/2496